JOHN HARBISON

ABU GHRAIB

FOR CELLO AND PIANO

"Abu Ghraib" was commissioned by the Rockport Chamber Music Festival

*This piece was made possible by a grant from the
Jebediah Foundation / New Music Commissions*

*First performance: Rhonda Rider, violoncello and David Deveau, piano,
June 18, 2006 at the Rockport Chamber Music Festival in Rockport, MA*

duration ca. 14 minutes

AMP 8257
First Printing: November 2011

ISBN: 978-1-4584-1182-2

Associated Music Publishers, Inc.

DISTRIBUTED BY

7777 W. BLUEMOUND RD. P.O. BOX 13819 MILWAUKEE, WI 53213

Program Note

The title of this piece refers to an important episode in our country's history. Abu Ghraib, while inscribed on our nation's consciousness by photographs and reports, has been absorbed into the nation's bloodstream, its long term effects yet to be known.

The piece is in two movements, separated by a pause: Scene I. Prayer I; Scene II., Prayer II. Both movements begin in unrest. Later, led by the 'cello playing alone, they move into quieter places which leave the first music behind.

Scene II is based on an Iraqi song which I was hired to transcribe back in 1962, for a collection called Lullabies of the World (I was asked to transform its bent pitches and asymmetrical rhythms into "American family-sing form.") This song has melodic connections to two of our well-known hymns.

This piece was commissioned by the Rockport Chamber Music Festival with a grant from the Jebediah Foundation/New Music Commissions. It received its first performance, in Rockport, by Rhonda Rider, 'cello and David Deveau, piano.

—**John Harbison**

ABU GHRAIB
Scene I

John Harbison

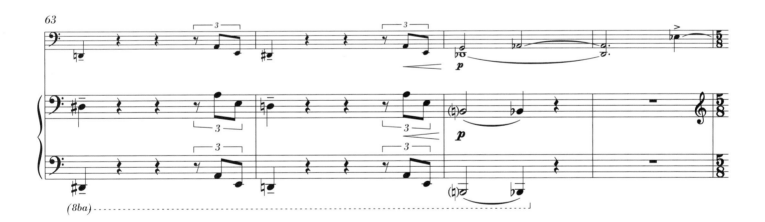

Prayer I

Doppio movimento ♩ = 84

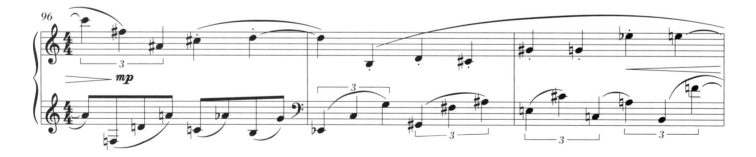

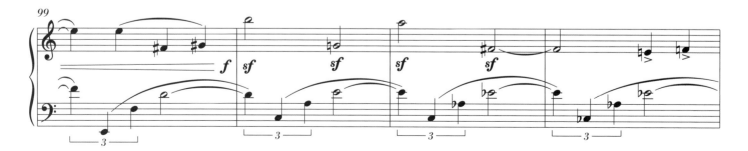

Tempo I (♩ = 84)

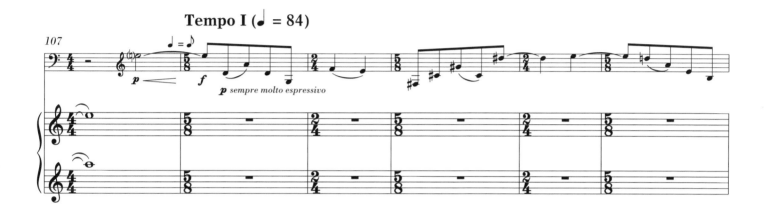

Scene II

Tempo I ($\quarternote$ = 84)

*In bars 12 through 16 hold each key down within its grouping unless the pitch is rearticulated, creating this effect:

Violoncello

ABU GHRAIB
Scene I

John Harbison

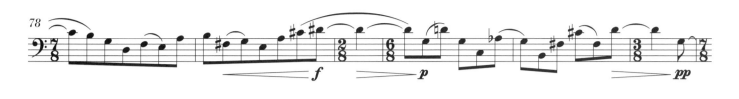

Doppio movimento

Tempo I (♩ = 84)

Piano (R.H.)

Scene II

Prayer II

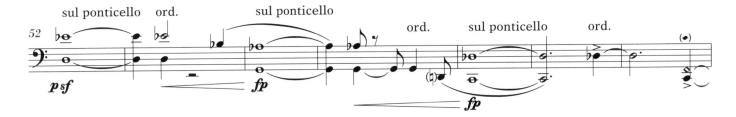

Prayer I

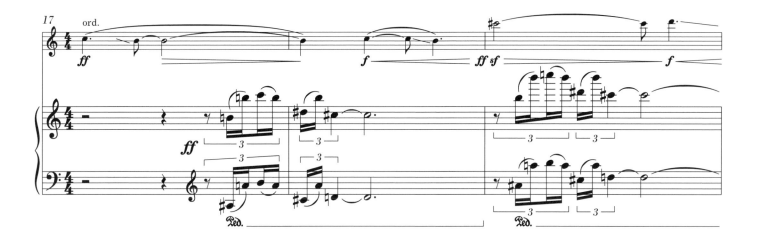

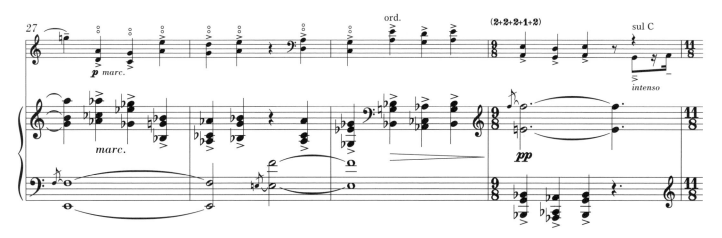

la voce superiore in fuori

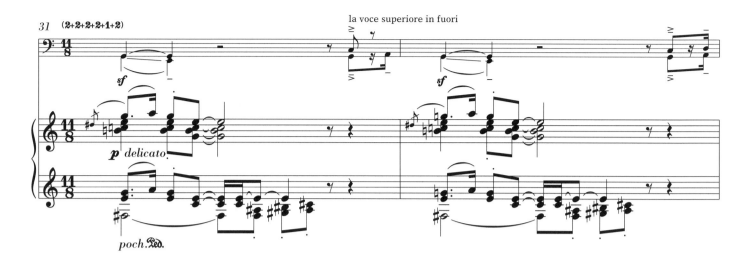

Tempo I (♩ = 84)

animando

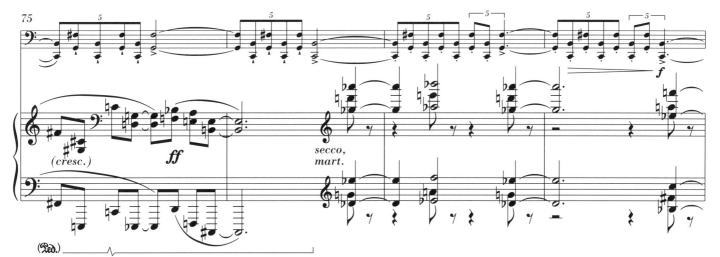

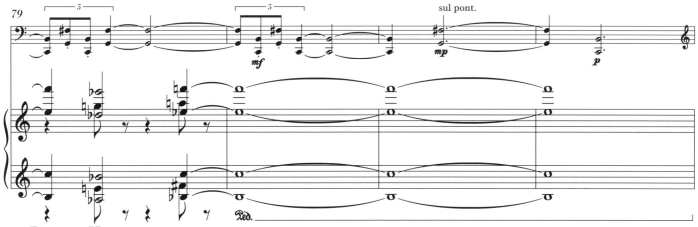

Prayer II

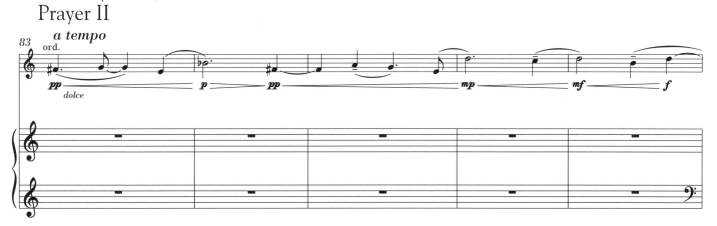

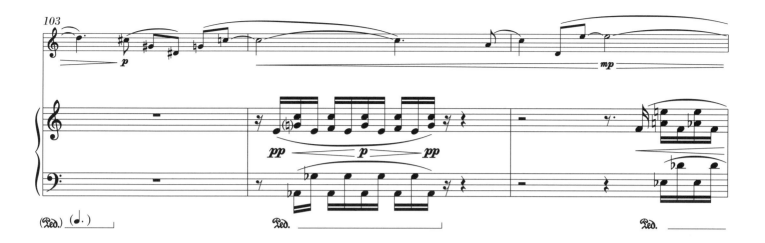

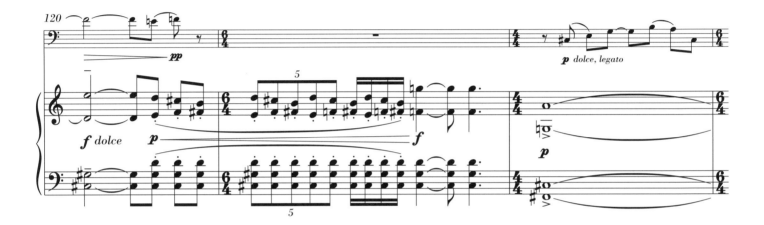

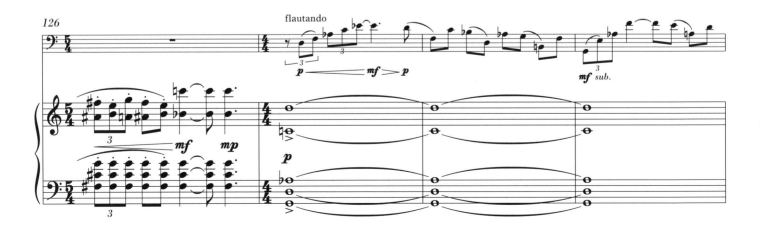

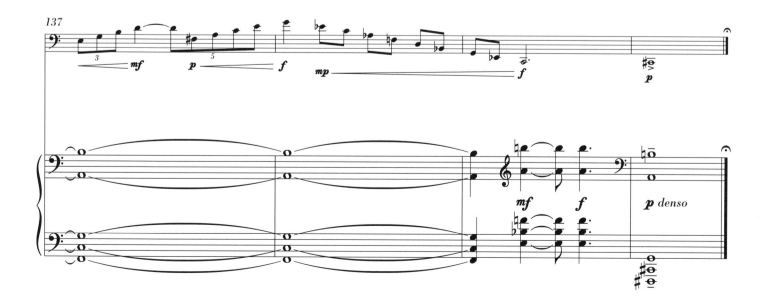